Old Stones
Understand

Old Stones Understand

poems by

Stacey Murphy

Shanti Arts Publishing
Brunswick, Maine 04011

Old Stones Understand

Published by Shanti Arts Publishing
Interior and cover design by Shanti Arts Designs

Shanti Arts LLC | 193 Hillside Road
Brunswick, Maine 04011 | shantiarts.com

Printed in the United States of America

"Leo Sayer Poem" references "More Than I Can Say," Sonny
Curtis and Jerry Allison, 1959, recorded and released by The
Crickets, 1960, Leo Sayer's cover released in 1980.

"Hemingway, Cohen and Bono Walk into a Bar" references
"The world breaks everyone and afterward many are strong at
the broken places," Ernest Hemingway, *A Farewell to Arms,*
1926; "There is a crack, a crack in everything. That's how the
light gets in," Leonard Cohen, "Anthem," 1992; "If there is a
dark and we shouldn't doubt / and there is a light, don't let it
go out," U2, "13 (There is a Light)," 2017.

"Pete Seeger" references "Over the Rainbow," Yip Harburg and
Harold Arlen, 1939, recorded and released by Judy Garland,
1939; "This Land is Your Land," Woody Guthrie, 1940,
recorded in 1944.

ISBN: 978-1-951651-48-0 (softcover)

Library of Congress Control Number: 2021932278

Contents

THREE ❖ Hope ❖

FOUR ❖ Daily Magic ❖

ONE

Nature

crayfish in the creek
rearranging muddy leaves
blankets for winter

under the surface
the forget-me-nots
wait without waiting

Billow

On the back porch
above a white chair of summer
there is a cobweb,
dust coloring it visible,
billowing in October wind,
undulating like a wave.

Peaks then valleys
Peaks then valleys

So much change in just
one windy second
fast, violent
like a ghost shaking its bedspread
and yet it hangs on—
no breeze, no bug, no trumpet vine
has come to release it,
to break the peaks, the valleys.

And neither will I.

Because each morning
at breakfast this liminal cobweb reminds me:
my life is, too, neither all peaks
nor all valleys.

Its change is constant,
though some moments are
surprising.

But I trust its rhythm

and I, too, know how
to hang on, dance,
billow.

Leaves Let Go

It is not the way of leaves
to care about how they fall.

It doesn't matter
whether there are heavy, thunder-filled
clouds overhead
or miles of bright blue and sunshine.

A leaf doesn't
cry out in pain if a harsh wind
tugs it from its twig
nor does it giggle with mischief if it
manages to break free on its own.

A leaf doesn't
fret over which is better—
to swoop down in a wild, swirling canopy,
a rustling riot of yellow magic with hundreds of others,
or to flutter demurely to the ground
in a quiet, private moment.

No leaf even considers holding on,
resisting its destiny,
its part in the inevitable pattern.

For the leaf, simply letting go
is the thing.

Harvest Moon 2017

Harvest moon, I have no tears for you.
no tears for destruction in Puerto Rico
no tears for shootings in Las Vegas
no tears for the earthquakes in Mexico.
They've all turned to weary grit
sifted through cracks
left by the groaning ground

Best, like that land, to fold in on myself,
or just keep running
or dancing
like a bizarre flailing marionette
There are no footholds,
the safe ground where love stood
has fallen away. Taken.

Gone to where
"thoughts and prayers"
have been swallowed whole,
their bland emptiness
not tasted.

On a fall day

On a fall day
I closed my eyes
and counted five things I could hear:
wind in the pine trees
leaves rustling
raven crowing
an elm creaking secrets
the air whistling in my nose.

I sat, eyes closed
and counted four things I felt:
slanted sunlight on my eyelids
oak bark cradling my head
tension in my jaw
a bead of sweat drying in the crook of my arm.

My eyelids resting,
I counted three smells:
remnants of mint in my mouth
leaves turning to mulch
a tendril of campfire all the way from yesterday

And I opened my eyes
to late afternoon light,
counted two dozen shades of brown
where there had been
two dozen shades of green only weeks before.

Eyes open, I listened,
knowing one thing:
what I would hear
would be what I listened for
whether real or imagined.

Ornamental Pear

The ornamental pear in the front yard
keeps its leaves, brown and curled,
until after the first snow.
It waits, drops them in untidy sputters
all over the smooth white,
while I complain to the wind.

My missed chance to rake them does not annoy
(I will not put on airs)
but it is not nature-like:
Buds. Rain. Then blossoms, leaves, sun and fruit.
And then dropped leaves. Followed by snow.

Who is this pear tree, stout and taller than the roof,
to pick his own schedule
like a rude manager, late to each meeting.
Or one, last, lingering party guest
who refuses to take her cue
from all its bare-limbed neighbors?

Nature in infinite grace makes her exception
for this pear tree, every winter,
reminding me once again,
to hold space:

some things just pick their own time
to hold on and to let go.

Mama Panther

Mama panther's eyes were wild
the skin stretched long over her shoulders,
solid, tense.
She crouched, waiting.
Panther needs the right moment to spring;
while she waits, does she
relish the tension,
feeling alive with possibility?

What if
it is her potential
that I now carry in my shoulders,
my neck,
my possibility,
my anticipation,
and it is only if I dare not to leap
that it turns to knots,
to aching
for the moment that was lost?

On a night of no moon

On a night of no moon,
still bright enough to see.

What if it is because we remember
we are all made of stardust
with our own inner shimmer?

Or what if we don't remember
and instead just glint like big snowflakes
caught in headlights
meandering on updrafts?

Either way, it falls to us
to create the glimmer
that combined
lights all our way
to the dawn.

Shoveling

What if
while shoveling tonight,
I stop
just for a moment
cease the stooping, stabbing, groaning and lifting,

turn my face skyward,
close my eyes,
hear the wind
as my shoulders relax,
the handle slack in my unclenched hands.

My ghost age six
rides in on that wind,
whispering giggles
into gusts of cold—
that breathless moment
at the end of a wicked sled run,
with flakes collecting
on my eyelids
like they did when
I finished by making snow angels,
just lying there,
collecting snow

like wishes,
like potential,
as they are
just now:

icy absolution,
melting away
all flaws,
all complaints
and infractions,
guilt, real or imagined.

Just so
on this frosty night
we pause and are
made clean,
new in the world
once again.

Time Is Not Still

"Time is not still," smiled hawk.

"You keep moving
  because you want time to fly
  and, like it,
  you want to fly, too."

How do we humans still time?

If we stop time now,
will the moments catch up,
become opaque
memories piling high?

And then will there still be time?
Or will time finally be still,
if we can just be still?

Cobwebs

On this warmest spring night
I find remnants of old cobwebs overhead
under the porch roof,
remember their magnificent billow
in an October wind.

Gone now,
just these tired shards to sweep away.

And I wonder
as the snake moves
along the bark, freeing herself,
seeing the world clearly,
with the film peeled off of her eyes
does she think to look back
at the old skin?
Does she even miss the itch?

Opportunity for New Discussion

The clematis—
too neighborly
to understand
the wooden fence.

Nature has no choice
but to persist.

The vines using knotholes,
and the weeds placing seeds
in the cracks of stone walls.

Sometimes we humans
prefer to resist

we pull back the branches
of rude plants that intrude,
trying to avoid conflict—so human—

where plants instead
see an opportunity

to begin
a new discussion.

Weeding

I rip weeds from the soil
like breaking old habits.

Some come up easily,
satisfying, if temporary—
I know I'll have to watch
for resurging growth:
old patterns don't die quickly.

Some have deep, thick roots
resisting a pull, they need
thorough excavation.
My aching knuckles caked in mud.

While twisting, tugging,
the root's gnarly voice
laughing at my naiveté
that some force preceding
me by lifetimes
would pull free, finally,
just like that
on one simple, sunny day.

But I do my best,
cut it off as deep as I can reach,
toss it away
and let it be.

Let it be good enough for this garden.
Let it be good enough for this day of this life.

Just let it be better.

Black-Headed Sparrow

Every day for a week I observe
the black-headed sparrow and her friend
in the garage where
they chit-chat,
hop along skis stored on the shelf,
perch on sand chairs hung high,
investigate the ledge of a steel beam,
their wings folded thoughtfully behind them,
little appraisers in feathery suits.

"You cannot build here, Sparrow—
think of this heavy, loud garage door
that is almost always closed," I insist.

"But why close the door, Human?"
their poppy-seed eyes plead.
"Leave it open. We can come and go!"

"We can't, Sparrow.
The world will see all this junk.
Thieves may come
and take the bicycles."

"All we see, Human, is all we need:
Soft rags with frayed threads,
high places out of the wind,
hiding spots behind thin wheels."

And they lean forward,
pivoting their heads
this way and that,
pitying my inability to see
the potential for paradise
in this cement
rectangular
box.

Solstice 2017

summer solstice eve
the stars hurry to put on
their party dresses

on the longest day of the year
flattened circles
in timothy grass
the deer are up early

on the longest day of the year
stone Buddha imagines
he can reach
the cherries overhead

on the longest day of the year
water snakes rest on rocks
by the stream
sun salutations

on the longest day of the year
dim congressmen in dark rooms
still refuse
to see the light of day

on the longest day of the year
whispered prayers on hilltops
more soothing
than anguished rants online

on the longest day of the year
towheaded five-year-olds
chase each other
straight into adulthood

on the longest day of the year
waltzing with the Sun King
lingering
in the rays before dusk

Cardinal and I

Cardinal and I
eat sour cherries off the backyard tree
at dusk.
"You're molting," I say.

And he tells me how he can change,
become even brighter
while staying completely true
to his very
nature.

Rainstorm

At thunderstorm's end
my friend the lonely cricket
winds his soggy watch.

Sudden rain shower
and somehow out of nowhere
I remember you.

Like distant thunder
I mumble apologies
too little too late.

Night rain lullaby:
thunder murmurs suggestions
for all our sweet dreams.

Well, Spider

Spider didn't wait when she heard the thunder.

As summer softly fell
she quickly gathered up
the stickiest strands of her web
and her carefully wrapped babies
and hunched her body over it all.

In the center of droplet-covered threads
she huddled and waited.

As we all must do:

gather our dear ones
gather our lump-throated hope, our humor, our tenacity
gather our red-eyed courage.

Whatever fortifies us,
we clutch it to our soaked hearts
and we wait out the winds
to see if we can rebuild here
or whether it's best to move on.

More Remains to Be Told

If you go to the sea,
go in pieces.
Scatter your bits
into the foam,
let them fall and roll away
as dawn breaks orange and quiet.

If you go to the sea,
go in trust.
Stand waist deep
facing the shore
as the shifting sand buries your feet
and the waves at your back surprise you.

If you go to the sea,
go with a child.
Fall in the dunes
to make sand angels
and hold seaweed hands as you jump
wave after wave after wave.

If you go to the sea,
go with your story.
Watch the horizon,
endless and comforting,
and know more remains to be told
as the sun sets orange and peaceful.

Two

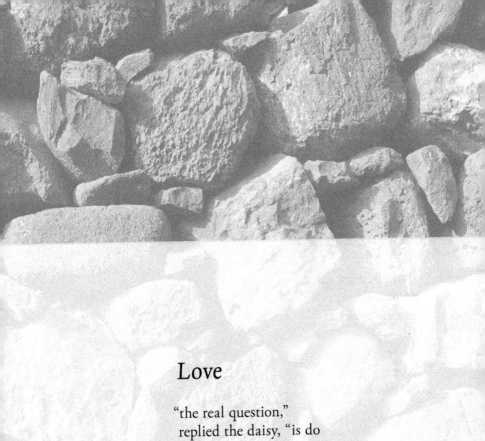

Love

"the real question,"
replied the daisy, "is do
you love yourself?"

Saucy firefly

Saucy firefly
winks slyly at me
before the sun has even set.

"You have no tricks
that I do not know,"
I tell him
as I chew an ice cube,
lemon-drop remnants
on my tongue—

sweet gratitude
already giving way
to tart longings.

It is more than courage

It is more than courage
that brings a flower forth.

It takes grit
to push past the dirt and rocks
on a leafy quest for light.

One cannot help but grow
in the right conditions

but flowering is another matter.

What kindness,
whether bees or butterflies
is needed to unclench a bud's fist?

How many tickles, whispers and teases
before trust takes hold,
and the flower opens,
full, fragrant, and ready?

For its patient, persistent visitor
to savor its nectar

at last?

The Leo Sayer Poem

Their songs spill over the fence
along with the scent of warm charcoal.
The neighbors from Burma preparing for a feast,
serenading me
and my rake
and my garden
on a fine April afternoon.

Now hip-hop, now rock ballad
my ears yearning to learn the words
in their own language,
and then—a song in English.
Leo Sayer from the early 80s
and we are all singing—
voices from their yard,
a really strong tenor from across the street,
my own among my weeds,
even the birds harmonizing—
we raise our collective, "Whoa whoa yay yay"
to the blue sky,
our hearts soaked in music
giddy with the promise of warm days to come
so we sing to them—

to our lives,
our people,
our universes—
our hearts so full,
we love them more than we can say.

Solitary Sun Dance

If moonlit nights are for lovers,
let the brightness of day
burn away my solitary discontent.

As I move and dance,
shake off hesitation,
give it to the King in the Sky,
my steps becoming stronger,
my hips bolder,
laughter and triumph entwine,
twirl

while breathless gratitude
spills from the folds of my skirt,
and weeps from the ends of my hair:
at last.
at long, long last.

Little inchworm

Little inchworm
tucked into bed,
the scent of lavender flowers
on his
ten unwashed feet.

Twilight at the grandstand

Twilight at the grandstand,
the fiddle player's sound check
stirs the hot air.

A ghost ambles past the stage,
another shadow runs to catch him.

Just a swirl of dust
to anyone looking,
barely worth noting
from the stands,

but we feel them —

the gossamer weight
of his hand on her waist,
the salt of his neck under her breath,

the dust of the space
still holding their dance.

After the wreckage

After the wreckage,
longing.
Fog that instead of lifting
grows stale,
settles deep
in our bones.

After a while we forget it's there

save for the way
it rushes to the surface,
meeting its mirror image,
its long lost self,
in the eyes
of another.

When a boulder dreams

When a boulder dreams
from its hillside
in the June heat
is it to imagine
raindrop kisses on its head
as it yearns for the next
thunderstorm?

Do dry August rocks remember
cool caresses from water
that ran through them
weeks ago?

Pebbles in winter stream-beds
know too well
the weight of ice above
dozing for days
until the tickle of melting
turns to fervid rushing,
the passion of the thaw.

Old stones understand:
whatever the season,
longing and its relief
are the same.

Bedtime Tuck

*—Bedtime for the ten-year-old boy. Twisted
face-down into the mattress, he grabs my arm,
which pulls me onto the bed too. Exhausted and
swooning in comfort, I settle into the snuggle.*

"I'm hugging your arm," he says.
"I'm hugging the rest of you!" I answer.
He replies, "Yes. And the sheets are hugging us both.
And the bed is hugging the sheets.
And the floor is hugging the bed.
And the house is hugging the floor.
And the ground is hugging our house.
And the core of the earth is hugging the ground.
And the ground in other places touches the core.
That ground hugs another house.
That house is hugging a floor.
That floor is hugging a bed.
That bed is hugging sheets.
Those sheets are hugging a boy.
That boy is hugging his mom's arm.
We are all hugging each other."

My eyes quietly leaking, I pull him closer.
"Yes. Yes, we all surely are."

Pocket Stone

If I could
I would ride in your pocket
every day,

merely a pebble,
worn all the smoother and more pleasing
by your thumb's caress.

I would bear witness to your moments,
your laughter, your smile,
that tired sigh,
lunchtime conversations,
joys and worries—

and when a dark moment came
I would help your day move easier.
I would be a magic stone

better than quartz for repelling negativity,
more protective than turquoise,
quicker to calm than amethyst.

All you would need to do
is reach for me.

The fields

The fields
hear the cloud's low grumble
as a tease.
Stretching out, exposed,
the grass makes hoarse promises
to savor every drop.

The skies answer, louder this time
and the trees plead,
"Just let it take a long while,
hard or soft patter,
these limbs will not tire
of the caress."

At our roots,
we can only suffer
without relief
for just so long.

Alone in these woods

Alone in these woods
initials scarring my bark—
permanent, excellent—
your fingers trace them
but don't feel
the laughter I remember—
the joy that carved them.

Breaking

What comes of breaking?
When a shell breaks,
we might see a bird, a snake,
a dragon or a pearl emerge.

When a cocoon crumbles,
it might be a gypsy moth that spreads its wings
or it could be a monarch butterfly.

When a mirror breaks,
do the shards reveal seven years of bad luck?
Or perhaps seventeen
different-sized and -shaped
ways of seeing ourselves
that we had not before considered?

What if, when the heart breaks,
we could find ourselves
holding on to our capacity
to love in the first place
and let Pain stand there,
right next to Possibility.

Let them shakily hold hands
inside our souls
where there is room for all of it:

where all of it really belongs.

Dia de los Muertos 2009

*— Tuscon, November 2009—inspired by the
All Souls Procession, there with my father just
a few weeks after the death of his second wife.*

That night in November
we released what was gone
but that we had not ceased holding:

loved ones who stopped needing their bodies
things that didn't serve
pets who still romped behind shadows of trees,
old habits.

And you and I, we took the slips
of shiny paper
and wrote her name.
I imagined peace where her shaky hands
and liver
had once been.

The acrobats lifted the cauldron full of papers high into the sky
and lit them on fire
but instead of falling
they twinkled and flew away into the night,
tiny prayers
on kites with endless strings.

Fossil

Is it possible still in this age?
To be found long forgotten, layered amid
brown leaves and mud
handled with quick excitement
but carefully,
your thumb brushing crumbs
of debris away, then slowly,
slowly tracking
my wrinkles and ridges
caressing the imprints
that have come through time:
not to smooth but to honor,
to wonder at both of us
taking pleasure
in your search for me,
for treasure.

Mermaid Tears

What if
the siren songs
fishermen were meant to fear
didn't come from the sea?

What if the powerful howls
came from the raw throats of
women on land,
women at home in their farmhouses
gripping the edge of the kitchen sink,
or curled up on the edge of the bed?
From women wandering the shoreline in shawls,
all of them keening,
mourning
for the matted kelp long gone from
their carefully shorn heads?

It has never been the mermaids
who salted the ocean with their tears,
that flavor,
little by little
washed downstream,
out of the eyes of those who would have tails.

THREE

Hope

the peeper chorus
singing out from the marshes:
joy always returns

Foolish heart, remind
me again that there is no
such thing as false hope

What if forgiving was easy?

What if forgiving was easy?
What if
overcoming heartache was as simple as
a long nap,
a float on a pond,
a few tears at sunset?

Would I
still cling to the ragged memory,
refuse to sleep,
stay on the shore,
swallow and hold my tears?

Would I
believe that pain proves a loyalty
no one demanded,
gripping the bars on the window
and ignoring the butterfly
that brushes my arm
as it slips out through the open doorway?

Leap Day

Magic in this extra day:

early robins greet this bonus sunrise
droplet kisses from the showerhead opening your eyes
a few more mindful breaths
a surprise joke on the way to the bus
and a song to sing loudly while ignoring bad news
on the morning commute.

A smile for a face that forgot hers
the scent of peeled clementines
the perfect crunch-and-smoothness of a chocolate mini-egg
a few more hours work to bill for
possibility smiling at you as it leans on the door jamb
the sun slanting through the window from just a little higher.

A day to get something right
to let an ache go
to receive forgiveness
and an extra bedtime to know
you did all that was needed this day.
No more. No less.

Scrub

At day's end
all over the world,
we lather the cloth.

Time to remove
the makeup
the armor
the magician's blindfold
the leather
the ancient battle-mask
the gunk.

Scrub through the fake smile
the nervous twitch
the uncertain glance
the bruise
the pox
the shame
the un-yield
the unintended insult
the fully intended dig
the well-meant concern
the sloppy unwelcome kiss
the piercing glare.

Keep scrubbing: try to get out
the control
the no way out
the making do

the not good enough
the slap
the sting of no choice
the scars
the silence.

And now, sister of the world,
sleep.
Tomorrow we start again.

Spirit of Fire

Spirit of Fire,
thank you for reminding me
to seek help from those who
light my own spark,
fan my flames,
or appreciate my glow,
even when I am just an ember.

Hemingway, Cohen and Bono Walk into a Bar

What if
when the world brings old breaks
back to our bones and hearts
over flashes of horrors,
our demons, and others' too—
we let Hemingway be right?
Recall we bonded back together,
stronger at the break,
even as we stumbled numb?

What if
we wake to know Cohen was right?
And recall that the light
that seeped in through fissures
fortified us, made us into
healers, teachers, allies
advocates, artists and
unabashed hope-bearers?

What if
we move forward, as Bono said,
into the dark we cannot doubt,
with lights that have flickered
but are far from gone out,
fiercer for kindness,
each day choosing strength anew,
sending up sparks,
giving thanks in the knowledge
we are tough enough to be kind.

4:10 A.M.

Looking out from the kitchen
at the arthritic crabapple branch
quivering in the latest of late night light

you think how cold it must be,
how hard to be an animal
or a person
outside in this wind,
and as you cross the floor barefoot
back to your dark soft cave

you recall that nature show—
the arctic groundhogs who shiver
as they hibernate
to warm up just enough to
neither perish nor fully wake.

How many nights could your
whole body shake and manage to sleep
through it? Could you?

What kind of raspy-shuffle
specter would I become on that sleep?
How long would it take?
You wonder as you
slide under the blanket
and the cat comes to find the space

you make near your belly
where he purrs and purrs, drawing
the shiver and gnaw

from your very core,
absorbing it all until
your eyes close just as they notice

in the earliest of early morning light
the silver outline of willow branches
appearing outside the window.

Pete Seeger

—New York City, February 2003

we brought our raw selves from all over
to protest the coming war
millions of people
seething through street arteries
young ones bouncing
older ones drumming

voices in all directions
cries to stop it from every corner
and then one voice through a PA system
soft and shaky and clear and true
murmurs and shushing through the crowd
it was you, in your eighties
you hadn't been well but here you were

and we tried to sing "over the rainbow"
and "this land is your land" with you
soft, shaky, and garbled through tears
our rage melted,
turned away from what we were against
to what we were for

our tears spilling what we knew in our hearts—
love the only thing real.

We stopped shouting
long enough to feel your
improbable optimism

and for a few minutes
your voice helped
our frightened multitude
believe

what had eluded people for centuries
really might have a chance.

First Run of the Year

Will the morning sun delight your eyes
as it glints off the dry
snowflakes floating in its beam?
The crunch of new, unbroken white
as you step out the door,
a wide canvas, cool and bright
between you and the horizon,
ready for your feet
for new tracks creating
the fresh semaphore of your story
for this coming year—
up hills, down lanes, snow angels
meandering down the side-tracks,
bounding down easy paths,
each crystal print behind you
proclaiming your way in the world,
this way in the world,
eager for what is next.

Hollow Bone

For something born in a dark season,
you bring a lot of light to others.
We try to be bearers of what we deny to ourselves:
hollow bones,
just a conduit for the light to pass,
to reach others.

What if
we were meant to absorb some for ourselves,
and use it to strengthen,
to brighten even more?

Even when you can't feel it there
your light gets through,
like a shooting star in the dark of winter,
and I have been lucky to see it.

Your Hands

Your hands, naked or adorned
spinning in loops through the air
painting invisible images
that bring life to your words
set cowboys and faeries dancing
in minds old and young.

Your hands, supple or gnarled,
stirring sugar into bubbles into magic
then wrapping dozens of caramels,
making dozens of scrolls on cakes,
for the sweet salty magic
to melt on our tongues.

Your hands, smooth or cracked
their own sensitivity for the details
our eyes might miss but our souls will not
as they sculpt, patch, mend,
repairing artifacts
rebuilding history itself.

Your hands, painted and raw,
children trying to match their motions.
Together you bring color to life on a school wall
just like you work it all over town—
chickens, boats, giraffes, bicycles—
joy punctuating the landscapes
of our daily errands.

Your hands, strong and aching,
nestling the neck of your guitar,
reaching for the rosin for your bow,
curled to tickle piano keys,
gripping a microphone.
Our eyes closed in wonder,
our own fingers reaching skyward

Your hands, worried or gleeful,
moving needles quickly,
yarn into hats,
thread and cloth into beautiful skirts
that your daughter will flounce
merrily off to school in
head warm, legs sassy.

Some evenings

Some evenings
all there is to do
is to press a forehead
against a window pane
and admire two groundhogs,
one big, one little,
browsing through clover
and take respite in
their lack of treachery
and ignorance of borders.

Some evenings
all there is to do
is to bring a boy
a spoonful of cookie dough
because he asked sweetly;
he could get it, sure,
but when you do
it can block the weight
of outer world hate.
One kindness
you can control
has to be enough for now.

Some evenings
all there is to do
is imagine rain
past the window pane
washing away mud,
sense starlight
coming through clouds,

so your heart can recall
it rejected helplessness long ago
and maybe tomorrow—
or next week—you will find it
once again brave.

To the Blank Spaces

What happens when we, who love words,
come to find ourselves more alive
in the blank spaces
between the words?

At first it seems like a clever trick—
a break from the flow,
something to freshen the mind,
to stop and attend
to the eyelash-lull
between two words.

The pause.
The millisecond between
inhale and exhale.
A little frightening for those uneasy in silence
to have any moment
alone with oneself—
best just to run straight past it,
avert the eyes,
continue the babble.

The brook keeps running
though there are gaps
between the stones on the bottom
where things live,
very silent, very still,
holding the winning poker-hands of possibility
while the chunks of ice and twigs
race overhead,

as fast as they can,
making it happen,
making the thaw happen,
making sounds to ease winter-weary hikers who
stop for sigh of spring.

Keep moving, keep rushing,
all will be well.
Better is coming, perhaps downstream.
Perhaps the next meeting,
the next speech,
the next therapy session,
the next story,
the next chat,
the next poem
will advance the plot.

But look closer.
Breathe into those
little blanks of white between the lines
that let our eyes rest
even while the greedy brain
tries to stuff it all in,
believing it comprehends all meaning.

Our micro-breaths add the subtext,
the backdrop,
as Paul Harvey might say, "The Rest of the Story."

—continued

Perhaps as we learn to notice the gaps,
so soothing,
so lush and full on their own
that there may not be another word

for a few

moments.

Whole naps,
whole meditations,
whole peaceful planets
come to live in the blank spaces.
I have loved and lost and loved again in the space of a moment.

In the SPACE of a moment,
not the prattle of a moment.

In the electricity of potential
it has happened so fast I have not even realized it,
the joyful rubber-banding
of my soul
playing in those deep true
blank spaces.

Auditory Hallucination

Willow at the edge of the marsh
wiggles her toe-roots in the cold mud
as the sweet racket
of thousands of peepers
washes through her branchy fingers
and the continuous trilling
gently coaxes the bark
from her bud-ends and beginnings,
to a green chorus:
"At long last,
we have made it.
You are safe to grow again."

Today my eyes feel best closed

Today my eyes feel best closed.

Such relief, such rest,
no harm from any glare or harshness.

Only the hug of a friendly eyelid.

No sudden puffs of air
or spiteful attacks of small print.

Now, instead, just warm stillness.

Gone is the relentless search
for papers, or keys,
or furtive glances through windows,

for people who could be there
but are not.

Forgiveness

Forgiveness is an exhale
Forgiveness is a blip
Forgiveness is a forced march
Forgiveness is a spider on the end of a thread
Forgiveness is a halo
Forgiveness is warmth returning to blue fingers
Forgiveness is a mask
Forgiveness is a leap
Forgiveness is a fox in the bushes
Forgiveness dissolves like cotton candy on the tongue
Forgiveness is the ghost beside you in your childhood bedroom
Forgiveness is in this moment, not the last
Forgiveness is a shoelace defying its double tie
Forgiveness is the last sign before the exit
Forgiveness is a creaking vane in the wind
Forgiveness is the rain coming again

Tapestry

What if it is true
that the things we feel so heavy over,
that the ways we think
we need to fix,
should have said,
or just have to rescue—
what if those somber, gray shrouds
of tar and iron
were not meant at all for us?

What if they were
handed to us only to cast away forever
but we misunderstood
and trying one on,
decided we had to
wear it forever, instead?

How hard, or easy,
might it be to repaint the canvas
of that story?
To rip out the sticky, foul threads
of that tapestry—

there are, after all,
vibrant hues,
softer, silkier threads,
infinite colors.

Summer 2013

As we drove to camp this morning,
the little boy noted the trees,
how their blurry passing
reminded him of a flip-book,
"You know, Mom—
the kind where you make the bottom corner
go really fast so the pictures move?"

And I thought how much our lives
are like that,
how this summer is passing in a blur.

If I could put a finger on a page,
stop the flipping,
stop the whir of time,
what would it capture?

A falcon in mid-flight over a trail,
lunch in his talons?

A little boy, mid-leap into a pool,
legs and arms ganglier every second?

The moment a raspberry
drops into outstretched fingers?

Please, summer, don't go yet.
Please, time, stop flying.
Please, me, just stay present.

FOUR

Daily Magic

bright first afternoon
I wait in the space between
my inhale and exhale

Chromesthesia

What if our voices came out in color?
Would my murmured first "good morning"
Be a mud of flinty brown and moss green
giving way to grayish mist after the first mile of a run?
And then, at the end of three miles,
would those same words, "good morning,"
show against the sunlit trees as a gold-flecked chartreuse,
as I call them out to the man and his dogs passing
while I stretch by the side of the path?

Would we see avocado
in the stories of the cab drivers?
Hear the neon orange and banana in the shouts of kids
tossing a football at the bus stop?
Would the words of the barista
placing a mug on the coffee bar, the words
        "Americano Grande,"
come out as sable brown or as a fluttering-but-dirty red,
white and blue?

Meanwhile, in the booth in the corner, would we see the
        peach-glitter haze
that surrounds a mother and toddler as she reads him a tale
about a bear and a piglet who are best-best friends
in the forest of a little boy's stuffed menagerie?
A collection much like his own pile of familiars at home,
where he will prattle in a language nonsensical
to all but his mother and father:

penguins who answer in the color of morning ice,
dinosaurs who answer in swamp,
the ape who chortles back in vine green,
the cats who purr back in mischief purple,
doggies who pant agreeably in joyful red,
bears who grumble in the brightest burnt sienna,
and the narwhal who responds in rhyming,
    shimmering turquoise.

Eighteen months later

—after Sandy and Irene

Eighteen months later,
they still stand near the Susquehanna,
doors ajar, empty
save the ghosts of the nymphs
that huddle and whisper in the corners.

February Sun

The afternoon slants sideways through the window
too bright for February,
trying on the purpose of June
but still it slides, edges, sneaks weakly
relying on its winter habits.

It finds your face, your eyelids,
as you doze in the big chair and it warms your dream:
breezes billowing the wet sheets
even as you hang them in the sun,
they pull your hands, invite a dance in the backyard,
the kitties around your ankles,
a rusty creak of the wheel overhead
carrying sails on boats out to sea.

Or maybe just one sheet sails to its partner by the tree
where the rope returns naked,
basket empty (that is enough for now)
the way the iced tea in the kitchen
will be enough to a dry throat
and the dimness of the kitchen
will be enough for sunblind eyes.

And later, sheets baked stiff with breezes and clean light
will be enough to slide into
at the end of a day after so much spring cleaning.

August Moon

August moon,
do you hear what's in my heart
as I bathe in your streams of light
your bright fingers winding through my hair
whispering like the oldest friend you are,
daring my heart, my hopes, my voice...?

You are the first poet,
the original writer of all songs,
the brightness we all want,
and want to be for others.
It may be the sun that sustains life,
but it's your glow that makes it worth living.

Brine

At the edge of the night ocean
crashing saline surf

rushing to embrace my ankles
my insides
my plasma

the cells that dance with recognition
sand over feet

hand reaching to trace constellations
toes and fingers

conduits of brine and stardust.

Our bodies mostly water
our bones flecked with stardust

endless vastness
above and below
the same stuff inside us

those glimmers we possess
nod in agreement,
reflect this boundlessness,
this tacit truth—

"Yes. This is your place.
And, yes. The dance is without end."

Young Buck, Old Fox

One young buck,
broken body
half lying, eyes alert, by Route 79,
the rack over his left ear still intact and proud
but not convincing enough to stop the officer
from using his bullet
to end the metallic noise and confusion.

I drive away,
praying through tears
to the sunlight, to a Universe
that might explain to him what happened,
help his soul to quickly reach
green-thicket-and-white-light-safety.

One hour later

One young fox
dodging into the trees
on the side of my running path.
red pelted trickster,
so afraid
in the midst of so much
green and gold protection.

Labyrinth

While only the stars watch,
I walk the labyrinth:
palming the rock,
inhaling pine scent from the trees
and worm scent from the morning rain,
the clouds now a memory.

The sky bright tonight
glinting off a shell on the path—
a shell.

And I smell something else:
sea beneath my feet
a mile down, maybe more.
the remnants of life before.
Bones of tiny beings
and giant creatures,
the ones who would have engulfed me
laid my soul bare,
divinely ravaged.

And yet here I walk
back and forth on the path,
into the middle, leave the rock,
back out again.

A slower unraveling,
the stars so old.
Their light taking so long
to hit this shell on this path,
everything winding back
to the need for patience.

Slave Burial Ground

—Inspired by the historical marker on Ellis
Hollow Road in Tompkins County, New York
near Route 79. It notes that 45 rods from
that spot, 14 people were laid to rest
in unmarked graves.

We had only the one witness tree
to mark the rods,
to measure the exact depth,
to watch the dirt cover our faces,
to mind the saplings that sprung from our bones,
to absorb our hymns through gnarled roots,
to whisper them on the breeze
and teach them to the catbirds
who sing them back today
into this line of trees—
a captivated,
captive audience.

Forty-two ravens

Forty-two ravens
circling over a house in Varna:
I watch and wonder,
in a week of foreboding,
what else is rotting,
has ended uneasily?

And then I see
the birds are playing.

Riding warm currents of air
on a mild October evening
formations gliding sideways,
cruising in patterns,
dancing together in the evening breeze
before flying off
leaving me to realize:

even the ravens
know better than I
to break from heaviness
to have a little fun
with the light left in day.

Dia de los Muertos 2016

What do souls do when not in this realm?
Do they play cards while waiting for loved ones to visit,
so they can soften
the dreamers' tired, worldly scowls?

Do no-longer musicians complete masterpieces
and jam out together
exciting the stars 'til they shoot across the sky?

Do souls marvel at the vigor in their non-broken bodies
while romping with favorite
doggie-souls in endless games of Frisbee?

Or do they peacefully drift, making something like
        soft breathing
that may or may not
reach back into our worlds and inch dried leaves
        along the sidewalk?

Sometimes our paths converge,
sometimes they veer apart,
but we are all packing for the very same journey.

Orange

*—Setting Sun Woman is one of the original
13 clan mothers, according to numerous
Native American tribes. Jamie Sams
writes about them in The 13 Original
Clan Mothers (HarperCollins, 1993).*

Setting Sun Woman
reclined in a field
of pumpkins and squash.

She watched smoke from dried cornstalk fire
rise against the low late-afternoon sun.

Her stretching body's energy
warming the very air around her.

Smoke trailed gently
past the clouds lit from below,
its tendrils mixing with those
of smoke from a distant fire,
lacing together, making the symbols
she had waited for:

a single, bright ember popped and
raised on the wind,
carried itself to that other fire,
her invitation.

She lay her head on a squarish pumpkin
and waited for a response.

Quiet

Quiet
frosty daybreak.

The crow
who usually
tells me a raunchy joke
cackling loudly at himself
before I can even respond,
is silent.

As are the dozens of seagulls
high in the winter morning sky
circling over
the meadow and this pond,
the hawk on her oak branch,
and me on the bridge.

We all wait,
trying to hear
the hundreds of prayers left behind,
frozen under the ice.

Yellow

Yellow, you are all at once
the sunlight on my neck
the joy in my steps on a morning run,
the trees in the distance,
the irises promised to me in the spring,
my will in each inhaled prayer,
each exhaled laugh

Yellow, you are
the lioness who kisses my forehead
and watches from behind my eyes,
the meditation pillow
that absorbs shakiness from my thoughts,
and warmth from the ground,
solid under my words
even as they stammer and falter
on unsteady feet.

Yellow, you are
an endless horizon
and on the days I can't see your possibility
you are lemon in tea
and a snug blanket
in a room painted in "Cuddle"
so I can see the brighter in tomorrow.

A Celestial Event

You might have seen it
from the driver's seat,
speeding down the PA Turnpike,
a flash through the moon-roof.
Then another across the windshield
and you made wishes
to break the dark
stretching miles ahead.

Maybe you were sneaking a smoke
on the way to the dumpster,
the garbage bags rustling
papery in the wind,
when a star shot through,
right through the center of the smoke ring
that you directed heavenward.

Perhaps you were already
atop a hill on the longest night of the year
around a fire with others,
drums, voices and rattles raised
naming them, welcoming them,
their light beings mingling with
sparks from the firelight.

Or it could have been
that you were asleep in bed,
deep in the slumber of childhood
when you heard the voice,
felt the kiss on your forehead
as if from far away.

In the morning you found
a bit of glitter
on the pillow
and detected just a bit
more brightness
in your mother's voice
as she slid a cup of morning cocoa
in front of you

and the new snow
on the windowsill
twinkled in memory
of what the stars had whispered
the night before.

If one vial of oil

If one vial of oil
can last for eight nights,
endure and light
and fill hearts
for seven extra days of hope—
well then, how long
can one shred of patience last?

How little space is needed
on a ledge,
for one toe to grip,
to hold the rest of me safe
until I can gather strength
to push off
to the next ledge,
and the next
and the next?

What if
the match that I am, nearly burned down,
charred, curled, almost no light left,
what if at the last possible second
I brush against one dry twig
that smolders,
flickers
and then bursts into the biggest
warmest
grandest
blaze of all?

Eyes Shocked Open

What if the frigid air shocked our eyes open?
Really open?
Cold clarity making everything finer
wherever we look
both outside
and within
our own selves?

Instead of rocking in the shadows,
clenching our eyes closed
can we bear the brilliant glare
of sunbeams on fields of crunchy snow?

Mothers say it is not good
to stare right at the sun,
but this diamond snowflake cold
has cast my eyes open
and I cannot look away,
will not turn away,
from a brilliance and beauty
that I once could not see.

Feed the Kind Wolf

Feed the kind wolf.
Notice her beautiful intentions,
prop up her sagging head,
whisper that it is enough –
your kindness is redemptive.

Feed the wise wolf.
Let her golden eyes feel your gaze
reach deep into her being
affirming that she knows
that better will come.

Feed the brave wolf.
When she appears at your hearth
move over, make room,
honor her courage
with the spot next to the fire.

Feed the playful wolf.
Dart with her through the bushes.
Chase and roll with your cubs,
howling in laughter,
whenever possible.

Feed the generous wolf.
Do not begrudge or reject her gifts.
Just graciously accept
and then follow her example
and give abundantly.

Feed the loving wolf.
Feel her breath on your tears
your paw against her heart
bearing the gentle heaviness
in this life together.

Acknowledgments

Many thanks to the kind editors of the following publications in which these poems previously appeared:

The Avocet, Charles Portolano, editor: "Black-Headed Sparrow," "Billow," and "Opportunity for New Discussion"

Hedgerow: "Auditory Hallucination," "Cardinal and I," "Scrub," and "Shoveling"

Painted Parrot, Zee Zahava, editor: "4:10 A.M.," "Billow," "Chromesthesia," "Labyrinth," "Leaves Let Go," "The Leo Sayer Poem," "Opportunity for New Discussion," "More Remains to be Told," "To the Blank Spaces," "Breaking," "What if Forgiving Was Easy," and "Yellow"

The Voices Project: "Mermaid Tears"

Gratefulness.org: "What If Forgiving Was Easy"

Wild Voices: An Anthology of Short Poetry and Art by Women: "Foolish Heart" and "Peeper Chorus" (Wildflower Poetry Press, Caroline Skanne, editor, 2017)

My gratitude also goes to Carolyn Clark for her optimistic, patient know-how, guiding the wrangling of these poems into a collection.

About the Author

Stacey Murphy loves writing and encouraging other writers. In 2018, she joined the editor board of Cayuga Lake Books and organized an Ithaca group to participate in the international day of poetry through 100 Thousand Poets for Change. In 2017 she co-edited and contributed to *NY Votes for Women: A Suffrage Centennial Anthology*, a collection about women gaining the right to vote in New York State and more recent feminist concerns. Murphy's haiku appear in the 2016 anthology *Wild Voices* by Wildflower Poetry Press, and her poems are in a number of print journals and online sites including *The Avocet, Painted Parrot,* and *Gratefulness.org.* She enjoys life with those dear to her and the abundant natural inspiration of the Finger Lakes.
— staceymurphy.blog

SHANTI ARTS

NATURE • ART • SPIRIT

Please visit us online
to browse our entire book catalog,
including poetry collections and fiction,
books on travel, nature, healing, art,
photography, and more.

Also take a look at our highly
regarded art and literary journal,
Still Point Arts Quarterly, which
may be downloaded for free.

www.shantiarts.com

CPSIA information can be obtained
at www.ICGtesting.com
Printed in the USA
FSHW021848230921
84954FS